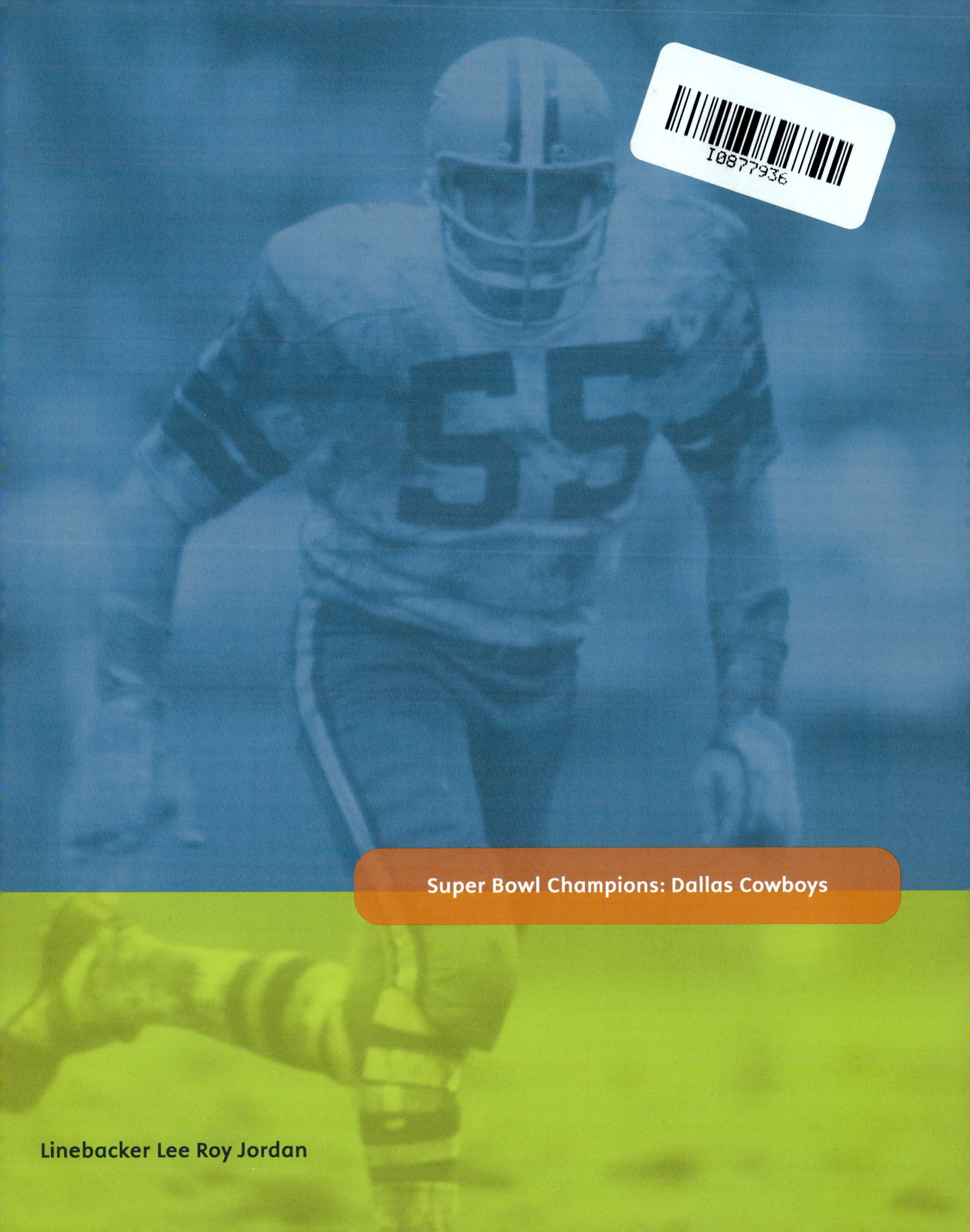

Super Bowl Champions: Dallas Cowboys

Linebacker Lee Roy Jordan

Wide receiver Amari Cooper

SUPER BOWL CHAMPIONS

DALLAS COWBOYS

MICHAEL E. GOODMAN

CREATIVE EDUCATION / CREATIVE PAPERBACKS

Published by Creative Education and Creative Paperbacks
P.O. Box 227, Mankato, Minnesota 56002
Creative Education and Creative Paperbacks are imprints of The Creative Company
www.thecreativecompany.us

Design and production by Blue Design (www.bluedes.com)
Art direction by Rita Marshall

Photographs by Alamy (Cal Sport Media, Tribune Content Agency, ZUMA Press), Getty Images (Focus On Sport, George Gojkovich, Otto Greule Jr./Getty Images Sport, Wesley Hitt, Ronald Martinez, Patrick McDermott, Ronald C. Modra/Sports Imagery, Tom Pennington/Getty Images Sport, Tony Tomsic/WireImage), Pixabay

Library of Congress Cataloging-in-Publication Data
Names: Goodman, Michael E., author.
Title: Dallas Cowboys / by Michael E. Goodman.
Description: Mankato, Minnesota: Creative Education/Creative Paperbacks, 2023. | Series: Creative sports. Super Bowl champions | Includes bibliographical references and index. | Audience: Ages 6–10 | Audience: Grades 2–3 | Summary: "Approachable text and engaging photos highlight the Dallas Cowboys' Super Bowl wins and losses, plus sensational players associated with the team such as Troy Aikman"—Provided by publisher.
Identifiers: LCCN 2021044452 (print) | LCCN 2021044453 (ebook) | ISBN 9781640263895 (library binding) | ISBN 9781628329223 (paperback) | ISBN 9781640005532 (ebook)
Subjects: LCSH: Dallas Cowboys (Football team)—Juvenile literature.
Classification: LCC GV956.D3 G56 2023 (print) | LCC GV956.D3 (ebook) | DDC 796.332/64097642821—dc23
LC record available at https://lccn.loc.gov/2021044452
LC ebook record available at https://lccn.loc.gov/2021044453

Linebacker Jaylon Smith

2017 Cowboys defense

CONTENTS

Home of the Cowboys 8

Naming the Cowboys 11

Cowboys History 13

Other Cowboys Stars 18

About the Cowboys 22

Glossary 23

Index 24

Home of the Cowboys

Dallas, Texas, is sometimes called "Big D." Many large companies are based there. So are many top sports teams. One of the most successful is the Dallas Cowboys football team. The Cowboys play in AT&T **Stadium**.

The Cowboys are part of the National Football League (NFL). One of their main **rivals** is the Philadelphia Eagles. All NFL teams try to win the Super Bowl. The winner is the champion of the league.

Linebacker Leighton Vander Esch

Naming the Cowboys

The team's owner first planned to call the team the Steers. Then he changed his mind. He chose Cowboys instead. Many people have ranches and raise cattle in Texas. Cowboys are tough and work hard on ranches. The owner hoped the team's players would be tough and hardworking, too.

Linebacker Bob Lilly

Cowboys History

The Cowboys started playing in 1960. They were not very good at first. Then in 1966 and 1967, they almost reached the Super Bowl. Strong-armed quarterback Don Meredith led the **offense**. Hard-hitting linebacker Bob Lilly made many tackles. Randy White took over tackling duties in the 1970s.

The Cowboys became big winners with smart quarterback Roger Staubach [*STAW-bok*]. He led them to victories in Super Bowl VI (6) and XII (12). He was later elected to the Hall of Fame.

Quarterback Roger Staubach

Quarterback Troy Aikman

The Cowboys were not as good in the 1980s. But in the 1990s, running back Emmitt Smith led the Cowboys to three more Super Bowls. The Cowboys won the Super Bowl after the 1992, 1993, and 1995 seasons.

Accurate quarterback Troy Aikman threw **touchdown** passes in all three Super Bowl wins. Speedy wide receiver Michael Irvin caught many big passes to help Dallas win the **titles**.

Other Cowboys Stars

Dallas has had many talented running backs. Tony Dorsett was the top runner in the 1970s and 1980s. He gained more than 12,000 yards for the Cowboys. Emmitt Smith set rushing **records** in the 1990s and 2000s. Ezekiel Elliott joined the Cowboys in 2016. The strong running back was hard to tackle.

Running back Ezekiel Elliott

Quarterback Dak Prescott

Tight end Jason Witten also set records. Through 2020, he had caught 1,228 passes for over 13,000 yards and 74 touchdowns.

In 2016, Dak Prescott took over as quarterback. He is a top passer and runner. Dallas fans hope he will follow in the footsteps of Staubach and Aikman and lead the Cowboys to more championships.

About the Cowboys

Started playing: 1960

Conference/division: National Football Conference, East Division

Team colors: blue and silver

Home stadium: AT&T Stadium

SUPER BOWL VICTORIES:

VI, January 16, 1972, 24–3 over Miami Dolphins

XII, January 15, 1978, 27–10 over Denver Broncos

XXVII, January 31, 1993, 52–17 over Buffalo Bills

XXVIII, January 30, 1994, 30–13 over Buffalo Bills

XXX, January 28, 1996, 27–17 over Pittsburgh Steelers

Dallas Cowboys website: www.dallascowboys.com/

Glossary

accurate — on target

offense — the players who control the ball and try to score

records — top performances that are better than anyone else has done

rivals — teams that play extra hard against each other

stadium — a large building that has a sports field and many seats for fans

titles — in sports, another word for championships

touchdown — a play in which a player carries the ball into or catches the ball in the other team's end zone to score six points

Quarterback Tony Romo

Index

Aikman, Troy 17, 21

AT&T Stadium 8, 22

Dorsett, Tony 18

Elliott, Ezekiel 18

Irvin, Michael 17

Lilly, Bob 13

Meredith, Don 13

Prescott, Dak 21

Smith, Emmitt 17, 18

Staubach, Roger 14, 21

team name 11

White, Randy 13

Witten, Jason 21